Your Muscles

by Anne Ylvisaker

Consultant:
Marjorie Hogan, M.D.
Associate Professor of Pediatrics, University of Minnesota
Pediatrician, Hennepin County Medical Center

Bridgestone Books

an imprint of Capstone Press
Mankato, Minnesota

Bridgestone Books are published by Capstone Press
151 Good Counsel Drive, P.O. Box 669, Mankato, Minnesota 56002
http://www.capstonepress.com

Library of Congress Cataloging-in-Publication Data
Ylvisaker, Anne.
    Your muscles/by Anne Ylvisaker.
    p. cm.—(Bridgestone science library)
    Includes bibliographical references and index.
    Summary: Introduces muscles and their parts, their voluntary and involuntary
functions within the body, muscle diseases, and how to keep muscles healthy.
    ISBN 0-7368-3354-4 (paperback) ISBN 0-7368-1150-8 (hardcover)
    1. Muscles—Juvenile literature. [1. Muscles.] I. Title. II. Series.
QP321 .Y58 2002
612.7'4—dc21
                                                                    2001003596

Editorial Credits
Rebecca Glaser, editor; Karen Risch, product planning editor; Linda Clavel, cover and
    interior layout designer and illustrator; Alta Schaffer, photo researcher

Photo Credits
Capstone Press/Gary Sundermeyer, cover, 4, 8, 10, 12, 14, 16, 20
Photo on page 18 courtesy of the Muscular Dystrophy Association

1 2 3 4 5 6 08 07 06 05 04 03

Table of Contents

Fun Fact

The shortest muscle is inside your ear. It is about as long as your pinky toenail. The longest muscle is in your thigh. It can be as long as 1 foot (30 centimeters).

Your Muscles

You have three types of muscles in your body. Skeletal muscles help you move. Smooth muscles help organs such as your lungs and stomach work. Cardiac muscles make your heart beat.

organ
a part of the body that does a job; the heart and lungs are organs.

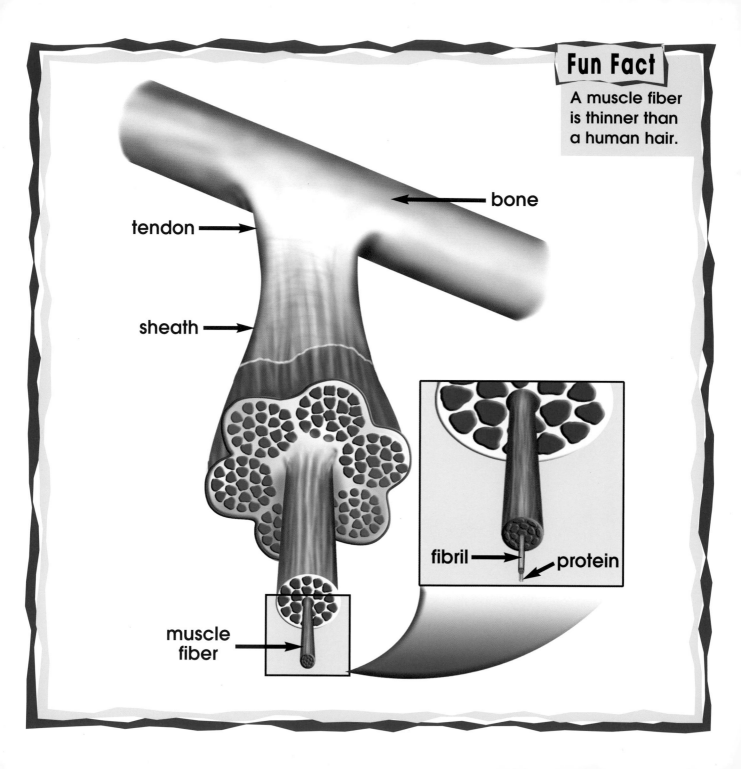

Fun Fact

A muscle fiber is thinner than a human hair.

bone

tendon

sheath

fibril

protein

muscle fiber

Inside Your Skeletal Muscles

Tendons connect skeletal muscles to bones. Bundles of thin muscle fibers make up muscles. Muscle fibers are long cells made up of little threads called fibrils. Strands of protein are inside the fibrils. A tough cover called a sheath protects muscle fibers.

protein
a substance found in living things; muscles are made of protein.

Fun Fact

Smiling is easier than frowning. A smile uses about 20 muscles. A frown uses more than 40 muscles.

Muscle Shape and Size

Muscles are different sizes and shapes. Large muscles help you walk, run, and lift heavy objects. Small muscles help you blink, write, and make funny faces. A triangle-shaped shoulder muscle helps you raise your arm. A strap-shaped muscle in your face helps you smile.

How Skeletal Muscles Work

Skeletal muscles work in pairs.
When you lift something, one muscle
contracts, or tightens. The other muscle
relaxes, or loosens, at the same time.
The contracting and relaxing actions
pull up your arm bone.

How Cardiac Muscles Work

Your heart is made up of cardiac muscles. Your heart contracts and relaxes each time it beats. These motions make the heart pump blood to the body. Your heart beats even while you are asleep. It pumps blood faster when you exercise.

How Smooth Muscles Work

Smooth muscles help organs such as
your stomach and lungs do their jobs.
Smooth muscles work all the time.
You do not have to think about them.
Stomach muscles help digest your food.
Muscles in your lungs help you breathe.

digest
to break down food so
the body can use it

Muscle Strains

A muscle strain happens when muscle fibers stretch too far or tear. Lifting a heavy object can cause a strain. Exercising without stretching first also can cause a strain. Your body can heal strains by itself. You can put an ice pack on a strain to make it less painful.

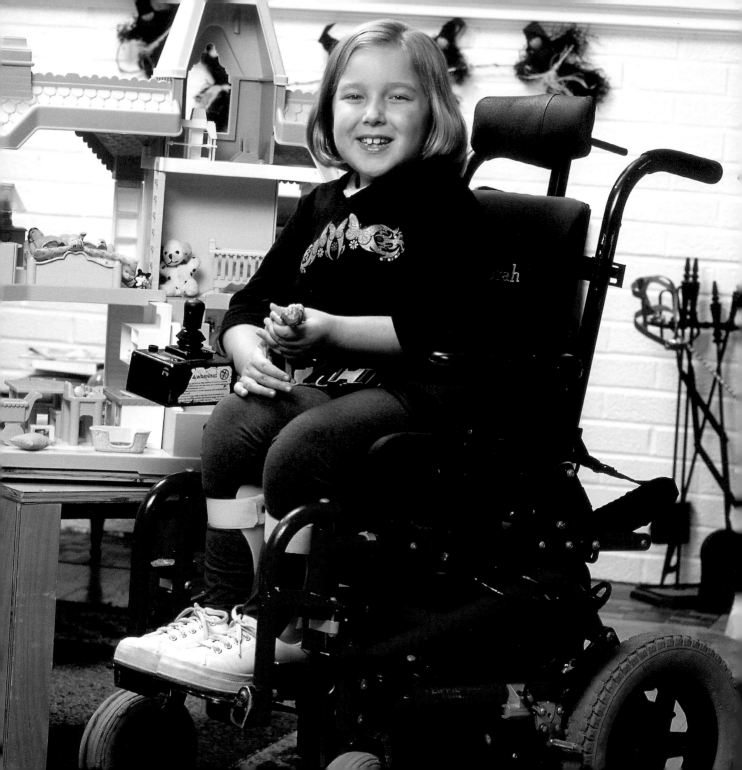

Muscular Dystrophies

Muscular dystrophies (DIS-troh-feez) are diseases that make muscles weak. Some people are born with these diseases. People with muscular dystrophies may have trouble standing. They may use a wheelchair or leg braces. Doctors do not have a cure for muscular dystrophies.

Healthy Muscles

You can keep your muscles healthy. Exercise makes your muscles stronger. Stretch your muscles before you exercise so you do not strain them. Muscles need protein. You get protein by eating foods such as meat, eggs, and beans.

Hands On: Watch Muscle Pairs in Action

Your muscles work in pairs. Watch a muscle pair in action.

<u>What You Need</u>

A mirror
Your arm

<u>What You Do</u>

1. Stand in front of a mirror.
2. Hold your left arm straight out with your hand facing up. Cover your bicep (the top of your upper arm) with your right hand. Feel the muscle there.
3. Now make a fist and bring your hand toward your face to make an L shape with your arm. Do you see and feel the muscle get bigger? It is contracting, or getting shorter.
4. Now repeat this motion with your right hand on your left tricep (under your upper arm). The tricep muscle relaxes, or gets longer, when the bicep contracts.

Your bicep and tricep muscles are a muscle pair. See if you can find other muscle pairs on your body.

Words to Know

bundle (BUHN-duhl)—a group of objects held together; muscle fibers are held in bundles by the sheath.

contract (kuhn-TRAKT)—to tighten and become shorter; one muscle in a pair contracts during movement.

muscle fiber (MUSS-uhl FYE-bur)—a long, thin cell; many muscle fibers make up one muscle.

relax (ree-LAKS)—to loosen and lengthen; one muscle in a pair relaxes during movement.

strand (STRAND)—a small, thin piece of something that looks like a string; muscle fibers contain strands of protein.

tendon (TEN-duhn)—a strong, thick cord of tissue that joins a muscle to a bone

Read More

Cromwell, Sharon. *Why Can't I Fly?: and Other Questions about the Motor System.* Body Wise. Des Plaines, Ill.: Rigby Interactive Library, 1998.

Parker, Steve. *Muscles.* Look at Your Body. Brookfield, Conn.: Copper Beech Books, 1997.

Simon, Seymour. *Muscles: Our Muscular System.* New York: Morrow Junior Books, 1998.

Internet Sites

Human Body: Welcome to Muscles
http://tqjunior.thinkquest.org/5777/mus2.htm
Your Gross and Cool Body—Muscular System
http://yucky.kids.discovery.com/flash/body/pg000123.html
Your Multi-Talented Muscles
http://www.kidshealth.org/kid/body/muscles_noSW.html

Index